Poems of the Messenger

By Rose Anita Renner

PublishAmerica
Baltimore

© 2006 by Rose Anita Renner.
All rights reserved. No part of this book may be reproduced, stored in a retrieval system or transmitted in any form or by any means without the prior written permission of the publishers, except by a reviewer who may quote brief passages in a review to be printed in a newspaper, magazine or journal.

First printing

At the specific preference of the author, PublishAmerica allowed this work to remain exactly as the author intended, verbatim, without editorial input.

ISBN: 1-4241-1411-X
PUBLISHED BY PUBLISHAMERICA, LLLP
www.publishamerica.com
Baltimore

Printed in the United States of America

This book is dedicated to all past heroes of my Creator and/or their countries. Who were willing to risk all for what they believed in. And to all unknown heroes who sacrifice every day for their families.

Poems of the Messenger

Spiritual	* 7*
Family	*49*
Love Poems	*75*
Native American	*107*
Political and Historical Events	*119*
Just Life	*133*
Thoughts of the Messenger	*151*
Messages and Future	*167*

Foreword

Sometimes in our daily walk we find such precious jewels of wisdom and spiritual understanding, and this is what I have found in this book, *Poems of the Messenger* by Rose Anita Renner. I loved her insight in the two lines of the poem "Angels": "Tomorrow grows from today! Every moment matters!"

Every person who reads this book will find a bit of wisdom that pertains to their personal life; a bit of wisdom that will make their journey a little brighter, a little more filled with joy.

I was taught by a very special Cherokee elder and wisdom keeper, John Red Hat Duke. His teachings are shared in the book *Red Hat Speaks* and so much insight in *Poems of the Messenger* adds to the spiritual understanding of Elder Red Hat's teachings. The Rose has shared with us insight she also gleaned from her many discussions with Elder Red Hat; insight carried down through the ages from our Native American ancestors.

Rose has a wonderful, close connection to the spiritual realm where she has gained spiritual insight that has been hidden from most of us. Reading her special poems will help us understand some hidden, eternal secrets of the ages.

I highly recommend reading *Poems of the Messenger*. May our lives be enlightened and enriched by the words of The Rose.

By Dorothy K. Daigle, Author of *Red Hat Speaks*

Spiritual

Balance

God/Goddess

Man/Woman

Ying/Yang

Balance is the Key
A good for every evil
And a right for every wrong
The secrets of Old
Let us begin with Balance
Let us Harmonize our Song
Vibrations from Thoughts
Creates the Music we sing
Let's Balance the Harmony

Male/Female

God/Goddess

Air/Earth

Fire/ Water

Remember Your past
Create your Balance to last

by The Rose

Colors

The colors of a rainbow,
      combined in pure white light.
The colors of a lifetime,
      shine out into the night.

The brightness of a candle,
      changing it's environment.
The rays of light penetrate,
      and the darkness is sent.

Now where are your rays going?
      The colors of your soul.
You are touching others,
      Oh, this much you should know.

The Rose

Death

Death is but a doorway
Into a brighter world

Where Peace and Love
Prevails and fills the air

Fear not what is unknown
About another place

Trust in He who'll guide you
Though your sojourn there

He can see your heart
Knows your True desires

And set your feet
Upon the proper path

Such a Blessed Event
The Pain stops
The Sorrow eases
I'm Ready!

by The Rose

The Golden Door

Death is but a golden door
Where true reality you find

The warmth of Love
Is beyond imagination of mind.

Let the Dead Fly Free
For so shall it be

Cling not to Life or Death

by The Rose

Loss

To lose a loved one
Creates an emptiness
Unknown
How to exist?

A part of you gone
Forever a hole within
Dear God
Help me be!

by The Rose

Doubt

A weed in a flowerbed
Can grow so fast
And spread its seeds
Then sprout its youth

Where will all the flowers go
Change comes so fast
As seeds of doubt
When faith runs out

Faith the size of a mustard seed
Can move a mountain
What can one doubt do
If it grows on you?

Faith is your garden
Doubt is the weeds

Let your flowers grow
Do not block them!

by The Rose

Fate

Fate is a lady
    Who wants her way.
A lady scorned
    Will have her way.

Today or tomorrow
    What is to be
Sooner or latter
    Will come to thee.

Negative vibrations
    Or tis fate.
Discern the difference
    Decision make.

Bow to the Lady
    Accept your fate.

Raise your vibrations
    Before to late!

You laid the path
    Within your past.
Fate is something
    That you make last!

The lady's mind
    Can change for you
        IF
You know yourself
    Turn your path new.

The Rose

My God I Love You!

My god, I love you!
Though the winds blow strong,
Though the storms rage on.

Dear God, I love you!
Though the darkest night,
Though til morning light.

For the morning always comes,
No matter how strong the storm.

Precious God, I love you!
Your light shines in my heart.
Love shows in the dark.

Wisest God, I love you!
Your timing so perfect.
Your peace fills the heart—sick.

I Love You!
I Love You!
I Love You!

by Rose Renner
Oct 30, 1990

Judging

"Take the beam out of your own eye
Before you see the moat in your brother's"

Man looks at one's actions to judge
But the Creator looks to the heart

As Jehovah said of King David
"He is a man after mine own heart"

It was more of a miracle
For David to touch the Ark and survive

Then for those who touched it and died
For it was but a battery live

The desires of the heart have more weight
Than the resulting actions of the mind

Yes, your actions matter so much
But what is inside of you matters in kind

"Judge not least ye be judged!" recall
Let's learn from our own mistakes or fall

by The Messenger

Jacob's Ladder

To understand this story
For two months I searched within

And when I found the meaning
I ran to a new friend

V pulled out a book of Hermes
Almost word for word the same

I was crushed, so much time searching
To discover His old claim

But if truth is within would not
All seeking Truth find the same?

A conformation I'd found
And the humbling not the fame

Then V "became" as Enoch
And Elijah's pathway lead

God is the same yesterday
And forever! As it's said

Jacob's Ladder, I'll explain:
How do you climb a ladder?

"First you look up
To see where you are going.
Then you reach up
To grab hold of the rung above.
To pull yourself up,
To step on the fallacy,
Of where you have been.
So you can stand
On the truth thereof."

We as Creator's children,
Are we not taught as children?

How do we teach our own young?
Fairy Tales, morals but truth lacks

As they grow they go to school
Less cushioning, simple facts

As the process continues
College—research, then they're grown!

Climb Jacob's ladder never stop
Progress toward the top as shown

"God is the same yesterday,
Today and forever"
Amon

The Messenger

Joined Within the Mist

The River of life flows freely,
Through out eternal ages.
As children of the inner soul,
Strive to grow into sages.

Through many times I've come and gone,
I've seen the River flow.
Yet, growth comes so slowly to some,
It pains to see them so.

Negatives of the mortal realm,
Weigh down the boat with stone.
Release those vibrations—Freedom!
It can be done alone.

For child, the River's always there.
Alone does not exist.
Together we float though time.
Joined within the mist.

by The Rose

Joseph of Artheamea

Oh, My love, my Special Someone
Know that I believe in you
Know that God believes in you
Whatever aspect of HIM you know
Believes in you!

Oh, My Love, My Special Someone
Why do you not want to know who you are?
You were my Grand Master in Ancient Egypt
You are the one who gave me the title of The Rose

I never turned against what you taught me
Even though you refused to remember

You were Joseph of Artheamea
You started your political career then
You don't need to prove it's need anymore
Yet it's not always the way to go

Your son rejected you Not
When He stood up to our oppressors
And fought back
Feel not rejection any more

The Rose

Keys of the Secret Chambers are Trusted to the Best

The labyrinths of the heart
    Show darkness at the start

The mynator within
    Must be beaten to win

The dragons of the soul
    Must be faced to let go

The sword of truth I'm told
    Will sear the heart in gold

Desire to be the path
    Is to become the way

Conquer your fears to grow
    The only way to know

Wisdom of the chambers

The Rose

Leprechaun

The Leprechaun of long ago,
Came with a story told of old,
Of a beautiful "Pot of Gold".

Climb the Rainbow's brilliant light,
Err not to the left or the right,
Climb to the top develop sight.

But down the other side you must go,
To reach the Leprechaun's "Gold"
The edge is close. Please go slow!

By The Rose

Libra

The hidden treasure of the stars
MY SIGN
My goal for mankind!

The time has come to weigh the scales
CREATE
Balance, do not fail!

Though Good and Bad blurs the lines
ANSWERS
Lie within the mind!

GO WITHIN!

Long ago the "Good" refused to know
That Balance is the way to go.

The scales were hidden to keep alive
The "Knowledge" for future mankind.

The pendulum swings to and fro
To reach the circle of time.

One must advance toward the other side
of the ball,
The straight staff to climb!

By The Rose

The Little Toe

Once my mother told me
Of a lesson she did learn

In church one day she heard
A sermon, lead her to yearn

What part of Christ body
Did she represent, her soul

In a dream she was told
That she was the little toe

Saddened, unimportant
Disappointed for weeks

Dad had an accident
Lawnmower rolled on his feet

He lost his little toe
Which is used for balance

My mother was important
She knew this ever hence

by Rose Renner

Look Unto God

When man fails to earn your trust
Look Unto God
When the Rainstorms never cease
Look Unto God

He feels The Pain in Your Soul
Believe in God
He Knows all that comes and goes
Believe in God

His Rainbow's out there somewhere
Trust in Your God!

The Rose

Prepare

Hear the sound of power
Feel the presence
Sense the surge

Enter not here alone
Use your knowledge
Keep the faith

Honor your God's history
Walk your pathway
Fear no—one

What's your priorities?
You stand up tall
NEVER fall

If Good is stronger
Then darkness
Must be spent

"Love one another"
What is this Love?
"GOD is Love"

But

It's says so much more
"GOD is Power"
Then
Love is Power!

The Rose

Silence

Still your emotions
Silence your mind
Feel your heart whisper
And peace you will find.

The still small voice
That comes to you
From your higher God-self
Makes life anew.

Rose Renner

Sleep

The soul of man holds within,
A promise to become.

The sleep of man sees no more,
The dream but deviation.

The desire to be—in the reality,
Of a physical realm,

Is but a path mislead—with no,
Captain at the helm.

By The Rose
2.1987

Solitude

Hear the quiet?
Feel the air?
Become one!

Envision
Majesty
Solitude

"Peace Be Still"!
"Still Small Voice"!
NEVER ALONE

by Rose Renner

Star of David

King Solomon took this symbol from ancient Egypt
It used to be called the "Mogen of David"

The word "mogen" means a mystical device
A device is something that does something

It is also said to represent Our Creator
So what do we see as we look at this star?

There are two triangles, a male and a female
These triangles meet in prefect balance

The female touches the ground
The male touches the sky

Become one with the Mother Earth
To reach up to the Father Sky

And if we connect the dots of the triangles?
We Then have an eternal circle!

Prefect balance, male and female
Equals an eternal circle

And this is the symbol of our Creator!

The Messenger

The Dandelion

Pick it and what do you see
A weed or a flower?
I see hundreds of long
Delicate yellow blossoms
How many eyes have beheld
Just one of these lovely blooms?

To comprehend the
Simplicity of the message
One must first understand
The complexity of
The one who sent it

See and perceive the balance
Of the life energy
With the death
You have caused by picking it

Understand
And
Grow!

By The Rose

The Sunlight to My Soul

God is so quiet as He works behind
The lines in the dark times of our lives.

We may not notice His guidance
We cannot see in the dark
Shadows of Hope!

We look for a way to see light
We feel so lost in the night
Fighting the Foes!

We wonder how long the dark will last
Our prayers are never ending
His timing seems slow!

But we will never be alone
God works on bringing
The sunlight to MY soul!

by The Rose

Where

Where do the Lilies, Roses bloom?
    Let us ask the Bridegroom.
Master Craftsmen here below,
    Take us where we need to go.

Ancient path though forest trees.
    Light drifting past the leaves.
Look up now and see the gate.
    Locked to those who are to late.

The Beauty of the carving.
    The Wisdom of the Art.
Contain Love from the Craftsman,
    And Strength from the Oak aged dark!

Though the gate we ask to go,
    The flowers beckon so.
There the garden blooming bright,
    With Blossoms full—day or night!

Peace that reigns within the walls,
    Overshadows us all!
I've seen the Lilies, Roses too.
    May I guard them here with you?

By The Rose

Your Life

The shape of a vine around a pole
A snake wrapped upon itself
The curve of an exit on an interstate
Smoke from a cigarette
Winding road up a mountain
Ripples in a lake
The circle, the spiral,
The Natural curves of life
They are a part of us
They are everywhere

Eternity—Rising higher—Change—Progress
Eternally rising higher though change
Progressing toward Our Supreme Being
Life is bending with the wind—not breaking
Traveling with the currents
Seeing where the river goes
Always ready to climb the next hill

Be still, learn, feel, grow, be real
Know life, nature, humanity
Progress toward your Supreme Being
By following your spiral pathway
Around the next unknown curves
Conquer loneliness, fear—Secure Faith
For you are not alone
"There is nothing new under the sun"

The Rose

23rd Version

"The truth is in the Bible
But the Bible is not the truth"
Words my daddy said.

Version: act of translating,
A translation, rendering,
An account it means

JOHN 19:17
"And he bearing the cross went
forth into a place called the place
Of the scull,"—Golgotha

JOHN 19:41
"Now in the place where he was
Crucified there was a garden"
That's not Golgotha!

Although seemingly instep
With surrounding verses we find
Words to consider

Matthew 5:39
"Whosoever shall smite
Thee on the right cheek, turn to
Him the other also."

Yet two thousand years ago
One who struck on the right cheek
Put you beneath him

While striking on the left
Was to say you were equal
What is he saying?

Let no one put you down
While walking life's pathway in love
It must be in LOVE

By the Rose

Moses

From such an awkward boy
You became a Man of Energy!

Long flowing hair of white
A smile that shines out in the night

Muslims, Christians, Jews
All recognize, your life in view

The time has come for us
To unite to become as one

Great prophet of our past
Lead mankind to peace at last

Guide those who can hear you
Rather it's Islam, Christian or Jew

The Rose

The Keys

Three keys I see before me
To become what we can be

Love
Balance
Unity

The triangle points of three
Are interrelated—see?

Each helps the other to be
Creating a soul that's free

"Ye must be born again"

As a babe in the womb does grow
You Must develop now know

As you progress toward the God head
Your growth will surely be lead

A pyramid is 3-D
A triangle is 2-D

So let us at least develop
The two dimensional one!

by The Rose

First Key

Love

The most important key of all
Yeshua Bar Yehosef's goal

Was to instill this valuable
Asset into mankind's soul

Greed and power of the first church
Robbed us, His inner lessons

Yet, enough remains to set straight
The pathway of this chosen Son

Let us: Be the Attitudes, use
The Right use ness of the laws

Love yourself first, then family
Don't forget love your in-laws

Grow outward to include others
Community, country—all

Now lets remember the saying
"If looks could kill". It's not late

What would happen if you sent out
Love as strongly as you hate

As you drive down the road, send "Love"
To those you pass on the way

And for those who have earned your anger
What I've found that works is: Pray

Once you can say that prayer for them
Your heart is lightened with love

But let no one harm you without
"Turning the other cheek" in love

The Rose

Second Key

Balance

A scale I see before mankind
Weighing right and wrong

If either side has too much weight
Scales are not even

Balance is an art my children
Learn to sing the song

Not Mister Goody Two Shoes
Nor one hoofs cleaven

The art of the tight ropewalker
Narrow be the way

Yet, a net I see beneath you
Practice makes prefect

Harken to my words dear ones
Hear what I do say

Let us learn to balance our lives
This world makes God sick

His patience can only last so long
And balance IS sent

Grace, love, taught—yet they're unlearned still
Do we give a choice?

A rainbow once did come on the land
Promise He had sent

An Old Testament God we crave
Less we have one VOICE

Create the balance necessary
Lets make the scale straight

Now walk the tightrope carefully
Fall not in the net

An important key, learn today
Do not be too late

Grace is love, balance, unity
The future's not set

We can lessen the intensity
That's tomorrow's fate

Recall Sodom and Gomorrah
God asked for just five

By The Rose

Third Key

Unity

Why does it take a disaster
To draw people together?
And the children of Israel
Took forty years to become

A Nation

They wandered though the wilderness
Bickering and in fighting
Moses and Ten Commandments
Latter they finally grew

God's Vision

Well now, we all know that lasted!
Still today what does it take
For strangers in a country
To work together as one

A Disaster

Why do we do this to My God?
And do you honestly think
That we are just a country?
We are a global community!

We face Terror

We fight for peace, not unity
We fight for money, not love
We fight family, neighbors
We fight our enemies the most

We chain Liberty!

The body of Man must be one
Your family, Your community
Your city, Your area
Your country, All humanity

Join in Unity!

By The Rose

Serapis

You still have the muscles of Hercules
A mind of a Genius
And the soul more precious than pure gold!

Body, mind and soul, you expect of
Yourself and others
So strict, yet underneath love behold!

From ancient Atlantis though Greece then Egypt
You grew, shared and taught
You are called a God of mythology.

But you are so very real then as now
Moses, Yeshua,
And I learned of you life's technology.

Your immortality was learned and earned
You give of yourself
So your students give to honor you!

by The Rose

Morya

Now how do I describe you?
West Indian, no that matters not
Immortal, loving, but you are more

For you are my dear, dear friend,
I love you, you can hear my heart
I was the Goddess to you for sure

I remember so long ago
Lovely Himalayan valley
I joined your order to learn the way

The journey to your valley
It self was an endurance test
Purity of heart—proven can stay

Now, you are political
You teach and guide those with promise
To direct mankind back to the path

Believing in humanity
You strive for your students to achieve
Their best and to give all that they have

But to me, I just feel "You"!

by The Rose

Family

Angels

Little ones at play
Growing day by day
Busy little hands
Busy little feet

Patience Dear Mothers
Trying times ahead

Angels are among us
Watching our every move
Learning to be
Like their loved ones

Tomorrow grows from Today!
Every moment matters!

By The Rose

My Blessings

The joyful sound of children playing
their songs
their laughter
their pleas for my time

They are the blessings sent from above
my hope
my joy
the peace of my mind

Thank-you Creator

By Rose Renner

My Children

I'm a mother who always leaves you.
Yet, I fight for you each day.
Yes, I miss you, oh, my darlings.
Children, Please hear what I say.

Tomorrow is so important.
I must fight for it each day.
But I miss you, Momma's Angels.
In my heart you'll always stay.

Love will hold your family together.
Even when your Momma yells.
I'm only tired, dear children.
We'll make it, that I can tell.

Just remember, I'm always with you.
Even if I'm far away.
My loves ties us tightly.
Close your eyes—feel me I pray.

by Rose Renner

My Family

When all is said and done
My family pulls me though
My children are the ones
Who make me feel renewed

They are God's answers
To any Mother's Dream
They are my only Treasures
Their inner beauty beams!

Rose Renner

Where's the Children?

Children grow as time goes on
Your young child's giggle
Will soon be gone

A young man/woman stands in front of you
What memories remain
His/her life though?

Treasure your time, make it last
For soon it will
Be in the past

Tomorrow comes as time flows on
Yes, your today creates
Tomorrow's song

by Rose Renner

M. Benjamin

My son
My eldest
You're so intelligent,
caring, so giving
Ready to help the world
I honor you
Respect your judgment
Treasure your presence

Your life was prophesized
Your youth enchanted

God almost took you
From us and this planet

God preformed a miracle
In your behalf
He gave back Life
And all you had

Dedicate yourself my son
To He from whom you've come

Your Mom
Rose

Troy Alan

My protector
My strength
You are a survivor as I
Gentle hearted, bright
A joy to live with

You try so hard
To please me

I wouldn't have made it
Without you

God grant you
Joys and Treasures
For all you've given me
May your life be full
To brimming with:
Love and prosperity

Your Mom
Rose

Charis Marie

My Princess
My Sweet Angel
You're so delicate

Your life has seemed so hard
A little mother at eleven

I want to protect you
I want to give you happiness

You're so determined
You truly could meet any goal

Never give up your dreams
For you deserve them all
Strive always upwards
Learn to know your soul
Please love my "little Princess"
Because I Love You
Never give up Baby
NEVER!

Your Mom
Rose

Olivia Rose

You Truly are Precious
Your compassion astounds
Your charm, your love
Touches everyone
Your wisdom, your energy
"Share with others"

You faced mortality
Before you could walk

At three you lost everything
Yet, so thankful for all you had

You always bring the Sunshine
"Never Stop"
You are my social one
You need people
"Lead them my Darling to light"
Your name means
Bringer of Peace and
Giver of Love
You've always been your name
So my little Cherub
"May you always BE"!

Your Only Mother,
Rose Anita Renner

Communication

As an infant we join this world
In understanding of where we've been
Communication we enjoy
For Light beings are easily seen

Time passes, we yearn to belong
As we age the world of light grows dimmer

So as my Gift I give to you
Communication to set you free!
Free to see, free to hear-To fly
Is knowledge, my Little Goddess Bri

I respectfully request the prayers
And blessings of the Light Beings today
To keep the doors open to you
Of this communication, I pray

So a token gift I bring you
Blessed in a circle of Light and Love

When darkness comes or confusion
Please touch this token to your lips Dear
Then reach inside of you my Bri
Open your eyes-speak-be heard-They're NEAR!

Your Grand-Mama
The Rose

Grace for Briana

The grace of a swan on a blue, clear lake
Gliding smoothly as the summer's breeze

Grace of a dancer during performance
Wooing the audience with ease

Grace I give to you, my niece, Briana
As a butterfly lands on a bloom

Grace of an angel floating in the sky
Erasing all of life's dreary gloom

Grace for all to see, Grace for you to be
This grace Briana Caitlin, I give to thee

From Aunt Olivia Rose
(written by Grandma)

Strength for Liam

My gift for you, dear grandson of mine
Is strength of character and strength of mind.

The Elephant in a Hindu life
Is known as a protector full of might.

As an angel ore humanity
Liam, guide, protect and always be.

In times of weakness, just reach within
Know thyself; call Mom, Dad or Uncle Ben.

I believe in you, this gift I give
Lead the little ones. Help them to live.

I expect so much for one so small.
Yet, I see though the years that you are tall.

You came here for a reason, my dear.
May the strength of Angels guard, no fear!

As elephants are never alone,
Know, the light beings are there, even unshown.

A toy elephant as a token
I give to seal this request as it is spoken.

I LOVE YOU, Liam Alexander.
May I see the day people call you Sir.

by Grandma

Angel Child

Angels are sent from Heaven above
    To wrap Mom's heart in God's Love

They Keep you busy night and day
    Laughing when they run and play

Independent—Stubborn too
    Yet—Precious moments with you

Memories too many to name
    Mine and yours alone to claim

Take your time—Let wings grow strong
    Stay independent—Learn right/wrong

Childhood is so very short
    Survive it! Regardless of Courts!

God gave MY Angel Child to Me
    We'll trust HIM to know what should be!

Your MOM
The Rose

I Miss You!

MY Girl
MY Child
MY Precious One

Tears flow freely down my face
As I long for your embrace

YOUR Eyes
YOUR Smile
YOUR joyful Laugh

No One Knows the Pain I feel
My Life now seems so unreal

OUR Love
OUR Hurt
OUR Needs

With Love,
Your Mom

Unjust!

A Mother has a need
To hold her children
On her knee

To wipe their tears away
And keep them safe
Every day

"IT IS BETTER THAT A
MEALSTONE BE TIED
AROUND YOUR NECK AND
YOU BE CAST IN THE SEA
THAN TO HARM ONE OF
MY LITTLE ONES."

"VENGENCE IS MINE
THE LORD SAITH"

SO SHALL
IT BE

ANY COUNTRY THAT PUTS
"IN GOD WE TRUST"
ON IT'S SMALLEST COINS
MUST BE TAUGHT
THAT EVERY TWO HUNDRED YEARS
OR SO GOD MAY RISE UP
AND PROVE HE'S HERE!

USE ME LORD!

EVERY child has the need
To sit on her Mother's knee

Who wipes her tears away
And keeps her safe
Every day

ABUSE CANNOT BE SEEN
WHEN YOU WORRY
KEEPING CLEAN

CAREERS DO NOT COMPARE
TO TRAMMAS
THE CHILDREN SHARE

WHEN JERKED FROM MOTHER'S KNEE
FOR REASONS OF
UNPROVEN NEED!

Rose!
(He is using me as now I am the Messenger, in hopes of
saving some of the innocents!)

My Little One

My mind is out of focus
Without my "little one"
There is someone missing
From my complex world

I concentrate on God
And the purpose within
Hoping for tomorrow
To see her again

Will she but turn away then
From lies she has been told?
Will her heart hold memories
That then will unfold?

The family reunited
Without our loving one
So leaves an emptiness
Blocking out my sun

Rose Renner

Mercy Louise

Your name says so much
My little one, who will never be

My arms will never hold you
Your eyes I'll never see

But this ache I'll carry within
Forever you're with me!

Rose Renner

Tomorrow

What are my hobbies, my dreams
You ask me my Hobbies, My life
What better hobby
Than the building of a Tomorrow
The hope of a world without strife

And what better way to build tomorrow
Than with the children of today
They are given to us
As diamonds ready to be
Cut and polished to a glow

Leave the rest to God
For HE is the one who knows

Rose Renner

Names

O is for Omen
L is for Loving
I is for Irresistible
V is for Valuable
I is for Incredible
A is for Angel

        C is for Charming
        H is for Hopeful
        A is for Achiever
        R is for Radiant
        I is for Imaginative
        S is for Sensitive

T is for Thoughtful
R is for Refined
O is for Outstanding
Y is for Youthful

        B is for Beloved
        E is for Efficient
        N is for Notable
        J is for Jesting
        A is for Ability
        M is for Merit
        I is for Idealist
        N is for Noble

R is for Rare
O is for Observant
S is for Sensual
E is for Electric

    A is for Amiable
    N is for Nice
    I is for Intelligent
    T is for True
    A is for Actual

B is for Brilliant
I is for Intelligent
L is for Loving
L is for Lively
Y is for Youthful

    S is for Sharing
    H is for Honest
    E is for Ernest
    R is for Royal
    L is for Loving
    E is for Electric
    N is for Nice
    E is for Elite

B is for Brilliant
R is for Rare
I is for Intelligent
A is for Amiable
N is for Nice
A is for Angel

      L is for Loving
      I is for Intelligent
      A is for Armor
      M is for Mighty

Rose Renner

Love Poems

A Touch

A touch can mean so much
It's what makes life worth living
To feel someone's love for you
Does so help you a long way
Toward making it though

Where are the touches
Of yesterday
Why have they blown away

Contact—skin to skin
A handshake, a hug, a kiss
Show someone you care today
I care—I love—I pain for
Where are my touches?

by Rose Renner

Come

If my tomorrow
Lives only in my dreams
Then I fear my desires
Shall be unbearable

Again I lie alone
No priest for the priestess
Unequal entity
Forever on my own

The full moon does beacon
Passion rising with tides
Stirring between my thighs
As I wait for the sun

Another day to come
Loneliness abounding
Another day alone
When will you ever come?

"Whom" am I screaming for
Out into the ethers,
The love of my life past
Or He to come at last?

All God's are but one God
All Goddess—one Goddess
All Loves are not one Love
Each shines unique alone.

Then what time is it now?
Time to go? Time to stay?
Lord show me the way
Or will He never come?

By The Rose

Day-Dreaming

Floating on a hazy cloud,
    Reality awaits.
My body aches from lack of touch,
    My mind compensates.

Hands to caress my waiting breasts.
    My nipples hard from pleasure.
My body swaying in sensuous rhythm,
    Feeling joy beyond measure.

My hands exploring all his secrets,
    My lips moist and wet.
My ache to hold him within,
    Screams to be met.

His arms wrap around me.
    His lips surrender mine.
The joining of two souls,
    Creates Ecstasy Divine!

by Rose Renner
(1988)

Eternal Love

Life in a void,
My mind in a haze.
The Love of an eternity,
Fades in but days.

Confusion and despair.
Where to go from here?

Back to the beginning,
To start anew!
Never to give up,
Until my life is though!

What has been,
Will be again.

The far distant past,
In a time long forgot.
Lies the secret of a love
That won't be for naught!

Rose Renner

Holidays

Why should we think of Holidays,
When life has left us alone?
No one there to hold at night.
No one to call our own.

But the whole world sings on New Years Eve.
On Valentine's Day the world turns red and white.
I sat alone on New Years Eve.
On Valentine's Day I'll cry all night.

The children will have their cake and cookies.
Our family's love will be expressed.
The love of my heart won't show his face,
After the activities of the day, I'll be depressed.

St Patrick's Day—the Fourth of July,
Don't bother me at all.
The lonely cry at Christmas, and Thanksgiving,
But on Valentine's Day most of all!

Rose Renner
2.10.89

I Love You!

I LOVE YOU
Hear me though the years
I LOVE YOU
Time has healed my fears
I LOVE YOU
The words we've often said
I LOVE YOU
The sound rebounds in my head
I LOVE YOU
Can not the emotion express
I LOVE YOU
It leaves me powerless
I LOVE YOU!

In a Dream

Then in a Dream I saw Him!
Where do I go from here?

He was the same one I saw
Thirty years ago in my dreams

Aged appropriately
        Salt and pepper now

But the same man
He spoke—He told me of Him

Yet—who is he?
I have no name

I know his secrets
        All of them!

I want no other now
Is He real?

Will we ever meet?
Why so much feeling?!?

by Rose
2.23.99

Joined by God

I remember your face in prefect solitude.
Eyes staring into mine.

I glanced down to see a ring of purest white light
Around us before time.

Out of the corner of my eyes—beheld a sight.
A man made of pure light!

Notice—Remember
"Whom GOD hath joined together"
In Matthew, my Lord states,

A marriage made in Heaven
Joined by GOD in light
Truly we are soul mates!

By Rose Renner
Nov 15, 1990

Joseph

I Remember:

    His arms encircling my being.
    My looking up at his face and seeing;

    His Eyes—As I swam into them.
    I felt so overwhelmed by him.

    The love that did flow ever so freely.
    Could melt any resistance completely.

    His hand moved on my back.
    Oh, but for the words I did lack!

    His fingers though my hair:
    "I Love You" I'd declare.

    His lips moved close to mine.
    His touch always so divine.

    He did fill me with such a glow.
    Joseph shall always be Beautiful!

By Rose Renner

Making Memories

What memories are you making
While you are with her?
What dreams of yours will she meet?
That I will never see?

Does she bring a smile to your lips,
When your day is done?
Or Perhaps she brings sorrow
For she's the wrong one?

My memories are my children:
And of missing you.
Now searching for a moment—
Memories still new.

We've made several memories
Over twenty long years.
Will there ever be anymore.
I wonder though the tears.

Rose Renner

Memories

A framed bouquet of seven
Four leaf clovers
An answer to a question

A ceramic sand castle
Made of dreams
Bought in thought of one

A baggage ticket from
An airplane
A moment together there

A couple post cards
And a letter
His writing signs, "I love you"

Memories, memories
Of a Love
Ignite my love anew

by Rose Renner

My Book

When reading a book
One surely knows
The end will come

Your favorite book
You love it so
Yet to read it
To live it
One must turn the
Pages as one goes

Some stories go
On and on
Others. . .

Look behold!
There's another book
On the self

Rose Renner

My Only Love

The only man I've ever loved
They say has gone away

I don't feel he is gone
For I need him to stay

The e-mail said he'd died
So then I cry, I cry

Thought I'd be okay
Until I said good-bye

I just don't feel he's gone
He was always there

My life will change again
No life Is not fair

by Rose Renner

Never Say Never

Never say never
        Hope or dream?

Am I closer yet
        Or a fool?

Oh, can I endure
        Forever?

Or forevermore lost
        In a dream?

Oh, tomorrow
        Are you real?

How can I get there?
        How to live?

Dreaming Forever
        For my hope!

Never say never
        Faith is Real!

Rose Renner

No Song

A bond stronger then life and death
has healed the past
and that will last

But today does not fit,
with all eternity
There is no key

This time around, the door is locked
The time is wrong
There is no song

Now I must heed the teachers
I care for my own
As you have known

You rejected their protection
Wanted not my prayers
my worries—cares

You need this life to go
in a certain direction
to see your sun

My needs are different
I must heed my teacher's song
I've fought so long

I must let go of my dreams
Knowing the time is wrong
Wrong for our song

I've understood you
Now you must understand me!

Rose Renner

My Guide

The night is dark
      And I am tired
My only thought
      Seeing your face

Please smile at me
      My Beloved
For your smile is
      My saving grace

I Can make it
      Though the dark night
If only you'd
      Be by my side

Alone I'm lost
      Barely half real
My other half
      Should be my guide

The Rose

Shaman

Dear Shaman, my love look at me again
Please reach out and touch my quivering skin.

Are you who you appear to be?
How do I bring you near to me?

Realm to realm is one thing good.
But touch to touch is as it should.

Hear my plea—fear not me.

The time has come to heal the past.
Love, it does not have to last!

Blue Rose

Someone

Someone to walk with,
Down by the sea.

Someone who'll reach out,
And try to know me.

Someone to talk to,
When things are too much.

Someone to share with,
Someone to touch.

Someone to lift up,
If he needs a song.

Someone to lean on,
When days are too long.

Someone to laugh with,
Someone to tease.

Someone to smile,
And put my life at ease.

By Rose

Still

There's been much sorrow in my life,
    For years, heaven knows.
But with one glance at your picture,
    Oh, my joy overflows.

Your smile still brings curves to my lips.
    Laughter heals the pain.
I still can swim into your eyes,
    Feel the peace that reigns.

For the so-journ between us,
    Thank you blessed soul.
For you have given me so much
    More than you can ever know!

Rose Renner
10.28.90

The Dream

Nineteen years have come and gone.
Since our beginning.

It's been so long.

Your smile lingers in my heart,
Your lips on mine…

This dream can not depart!

I gave up hope in my despair.
The road so dark.

Do you still care?

Rose Renner
10.29.88

The End

Almost a year has come and gone.
A new world I see-but the old one still beacons me.
The tears still so fresh-the pain in my breast.

The beach I saw again last week,
The beach, the sand, the sea, the palm trees, the shells…
But the face was not yours..
The words were not yours…

The gulf called to me-to come out into the sea
Forever to be free!
It pulled at my feet-the voice was so sweet
But my children-I need to keep.

I cannot live the life you want for me.
I cannot let my dreams die
What I saw in your eyes was not a lie

So two worlds I will weave though
Praying for a door from you.

Rose Renner
"8.25.86"

The Eyes

The eyes are the mirror of the soul
The soul speaks it's own language
The soul speaks only of truth

The Aura is vibrations from thought
As pebbles dropped in a pond
Send ringlets out to it's shore

I know the circumstances you face
Yet was the truth in your eyes
It was the love of your youth

I feel the vibrations of your thoughts
I see not their beautiful colors
My arms caressed beg for more

Your eyes, your aura match not your words
Pain from your words—unbearable\
Clouds my knowing—confusion

Latter in my memory—your eyes
Your aura so real touched me
I will try understanding.

Rose
July 1990

The Sun

How do you tell the sun not to shine?
Sometimes it's cloudy
Sometimes you hide under a tree from the heat
Sometimes it's night and you can not find the suns light anywhere
All that's there is it's shadow, the moon
Sometimes in the night you stumble and fall
Sometimes the noises frighten you and the shadows,
The thorns and rocks can hurt
But the light always comes back
Sometimes you run indoors because the sunburn hurts
There's only artificial light there
It's not as warm
Sometimes you look for a doorway to another world
Where the sun is always there and warm and you are safe
From all—no rocks—no thorns
And the sun doesn't burn you
How do you find a doorway to another world
When you only know one sun?

Two years ago I ran away, I was afraid of my hurts
I hid in the caves, it is dark here
The few times I have found light, it was not real
There are strange noises and shadows and rocks here
I need my sun
I dream of it's warmth
I remember the beauty of it's light upon the spring flowers
But, I am lost in my cave
I need a ray of sunlight to follow to find my way out

I can not ask my sun not to shine, I need its warmth
I need it's light, I fear being alone

Rose (Oct 30,88)

The Gift

Learn what you can,
When "The Fates" bring us together,
For tomorrow you may see
A different day.

Learn what you can,
To be a better man.
Take the Treasures of "The Goddess"
Caress them with your hand.

This "Gift" she has given
Is given but for a time.
Life holds many lessons, though
I may want to make you mine.

I'm a servant of "The Goddess".
Her hand leads my way.
So learn what you can.
Be ready for your new day!

Tomorrow holds another.
Who may never leave your side.
Let me help prepare you,
To be ready to be her guide.

By The Rose

Together

From a time before time
To a future without end

My love steadily grows
For my lover, my friend

One lifetime is so short
Just a moment in time
Rather close or apart
We will both make the climb

Rose Renner

What Is Loney?

I miss you, My LOVE.
I am so lonely now.

        Another day is dawning.
        Another night is though.

I ache for peace, My Love.
I ache so deep within my soul.

        Another day is dawning.
        Another night is though.

        My need for you is stronger.
        As a flower needs the dew.

I miss you, My LOVE.
I am so lonely now.

Rose Renner
11.24.85

Where Is My Dream?

Resting on the restless SEA OF DESIRE,
The sensations of my lower senses
Creating havoc-flaming my fire.

Quivering of my body aching within,
Needs, never to be met will come again.
Mind strong enough to control, If not touched!

Fear of opening up to someone new.
A woman alone in a world of men.
Loneliness racks my body as the flu.

The whistles, the horns, the double takes, the stares,
The offers are plenty to quench the fire.
But just one—is all I desire.

One man to caress my quivering skin,
To part my lips—feel the heat within!
One to stay—keep ALL others away.

Oh, but to dream and feel his velvet touch.
How else to ever achieve so much?
Fear—Pain—Need—Loneliness—Desire-
HOT FIRE!

Where is my dream?

By Rose Renner

Whom God Hath Joined Together

"Whom GOD hath joined together,
    Let no man put asunder." (Matt 19:6)
What just man joins together,
    Usually goes a blunder.
Beware my little children,
    You must look for your twin flame.
A helpmate to stand beside you,
    Creates two minds that work the same.
The journey may be tedious,
    To completely prepare the way.
The time may pass so slowly.
    But please, hear me, what I say.
Listen to me, my dear children.
    You must learn to be like the dove.
Now follow your inner rainbow
    In your heart's pathway of True Love!

By The Rose
August 8, 1987

Native Americans

Hopi

The Hopi with their treasured past
You're my dear children

So much fear, tomorrow's judgment
Yet faithful, my friends

You have truly lost your head
Chief Mike was the last

So much history and so much heart
Guardians hold fast

Faithfulness is always noticed
Remember King David

Nathen said he should have been stoned
The Creator said

"He's a man after my own heart"
Your God looks within

by Blue Rose

Cherokee

Artists, musicians
Intelligent, cultured
Clan mothers, Elders
Medicine men/women
Community

White Man Came

Your world shrinks
New Echota developed
Alphabet, newspaper
Legislature, delegates
Farmsteads

Trail of Tears

Reservations or hiding, fear
Restrictions, poor schools
Hopelessness, alcohol,
"Who are we?"
"I don't know!"

Tomorrow

Keetoowah lead the way!
Descendants of Keturah and Israel
Seven tribes to America
The Elders fasted
Cherokee is the Chief Nation

Great wakening, Revival
Thank You Red Hat

by Blue Rose

To the Lakota

She came to you so long ago
To tell of Hope
Though "The White Buffaloe"

If She should return this very day
Would you be ready?
Or turn away?

The white man's world you fell into
Is it not choking?
And smothering you?

This true balance that you once knew
Does only come
From inside you

As a culture grows from within
Ones learns it can not be
As surface skin

I "remember" the past—I care!
How do I awaken
This "Sleeping Bear?"

Blue Rose

To My Sons and My Daughters

Where are your brothers?
Where are your sisters?

Are we not all one?
My children, My relations?

One family in this place
We grow, we learn, we fight!

Hear your parents.
Feel their sorrow.

You are brothers.
You are sisters.

The night is falling.
Tomorrow is the light!

Be one with The Mother,
"Ground with her."

Reach up to The Father,
"Let us rise!"

by Blue Rose

Sisters

Long ago in a pre Mayan world
Five shamans dealt as one

They knew the plants, roots to heal their own
Ladies under the sun

In a cave they dwelt in the rain forest
As one with earth and sky

From the city of gold they'd journey
Seeking our knowledge, why?

We were their healers, guides; the journey
Proved those worthy in light

Today

I have found three of my sisters here
Working for mankind's fight

We each walk our own pathway, yet
Our fight of the same wrath

Where is my fourth sister? I wonder.
Somewhere walking her path

The dark one we will help to abolish
His day will turn to night!

We in our own ways help guide mankind
Back to Creator's LIGHT!

Blue Rose

The Spirit of the Wind

You feel me. I am everywhere
I come unseen, I move trees

I can destroy you
Or
Keep you cool as a gentle breeze

I feel you
Your pain, confusion
Your pride, your greed
Your need for power

We are one
We need each other

First be one with the Mother
Then
Rise to Father Sky

As the Eagle flies upon the wind
As lightening lights a stormy night

You can soar in harmony and peace
Unite and forget the fight

The Cherokee of long ago
Developed community

Together they raised the young
To honor and to be one

Even as the wind blows
The Willow will not break

Remember who you are
It is never too late

By Blue Rose

Political and Historical Events

History

"Study to show thyself approved"
It was written as it wasn't
Accuracy in history
I do NOT see!

Truths are hidden or altered there
They must be found through searching
Many sources of material
For truth to be

Is it not time for us to see
True history as it should be?
The future depends on us
It is a must!

The temple of Alexandria
I see again as it was
The true history of mankind
It did contain

By The Rose

Desert Shield

Or the night before any battle

The desert's so cold
The night's so long
The minutes tick by so slowly

With the deadline so near
I wonder who will
Survive to arrive back home

My buddy beside me
Asleep on his bunk
A friend over in the next tent

We have the same dreams
Share the same fear
But our courage shall never
Be Bend!

by Rose Renner

Dunbane

Remember me, Mother
    Remember my laugh!
Remember me, Father,
    As I'd reach for your hand!

Remember me, my eyes,
    How they'd sparkle-shine.
Remember me—Christmas
    All the joys I'd find.

Remember me—Dunblane
    Do forget your pain.
Remember me—Scotland,
    Help my friends smile again.

    Remember Me
    REMEMBER US

We will always remember you!

By The Rose

Elian

Elian, forgive America
The Land of The Free
For We Know Not What We do

Castro, someone we don't understand
Compared to Hitler??
Who remembers World War II?

A Jewish Child in your place back then
Would We have returned?
Castro, dictator = no choices!

Yes, Cubans are passionate
BUT Intelligent!
Why can't we hear their voices?

Will They use your notoriety?
International Politics
Are we too late?

America hear my plea, LISTEN
He's just a Baby
And we are his only DREAM!

Juan Miguel has family There
Can he freely speak?
Or are things NOT as they seem?

The AMERICAN FLAG belongs
To ALL AMERICANS
Even to Cuban ones!

By The Rose

September 11, 2001

Shock, fear, I have to get out!
A strength from within
Feel though the smoke
An Angelic presence

"No never alone"
A song I learned as a child
"He promised never to leave me
Never to leave me alone"

God kept His promise
That September day.
The buildings were filled
With angels guiding the way

America was warned
Know this my children
A vision was sent
To HIS messenger

"In God We Trust"
Written on our smallest coins
Cannot penetrate
The minds in control

Then balance came
When they refused to Obey
Why cannot they listen?
To what my GOD did say?

HE gave them two commands
To stop wearing HIS shoes.
1.Get out of the American family
2.And in something else, concerning research.

Now we see "they've
Created life in the form
Of a deadly Virus
And published the means!

Maybe He's trying to save us
From our own stupidity
Ah, what else are "they" doing?
This is lucidity!

All summer the messenger prayed
The White House was saved
The plane was delayed
Filled with our best

But the pentagon
And the place where greed grew
Is there not a message here?
Can we learn?

GOD kept His promise
That September day
The buildings were filled
With angels guiding the way

No, Never Alone
In GOD we Trust

It is never too late to Obey
Just ask Him to show the way!
Give a token
"Trust and Obey"

By The Messenger

America, America

America, America
Lift up your head behold
The God above is filled with Love
And hears your every prayer.

Fear not Dear land, From His strong hand
He'll bring the peace you need.
His balance comes within His Love.
Bow down your head and heed.

The Messenger

Bin Laden

Osama, some believe you are a prophet
    You believe we are the great Satan

Yahweh always uses His children's enemies
    Yes, to bring them back into His hand

You say this war is a jihad of Allah
    I say it's judgment from Gabriel

When mankind returns to their Supreme Being
    Only then will peace reign, hate unravel

The descendants of Ishmael and Isaac
    Will one day hold hands again in love

Then will you release your hatred Osama
    Mohammad ceased his jihad can you?

If you are truly a servant of Allah
    Then you will hear the song of His dove

The western world does not believe you are His
    They've been taught of grace. They have no clue

All have forgotten the Israelites history
    Balance still comes to all, even you

I judge not, Nor do I condone your actions
    This world, everyone has much to learn

I pray for balance, lessons are needed
    But how can you hurt others, discern

The Messenger

Hurricane Isabel

A hurricane is on the way
Toward Washington they say

Power of Yahweh they should see
Potomac a path should be

Gabriel: "No, west it should go".
Words he wanted me to know

"To frighten them"
"To slow down their research!"?

Strange He rarely speaks to me
How important this must be!

Where is this research, I wonder?
What is sanctioned, I ponder?

Afterwards, Fort Derrick it is!
A sinkhole under the rails

Now this would slow down a train
Is this where? What do they gain?

by the Messenger

Just Life

What is "___?"

In a barnyard I once did tread
And placed my foot in that well dread

The smell obtrusive to my nose
As it oozed up between my toes

Later in life "___" slipped from my lips
And then with hands upon my hips

"Is this a cuss word I spoke out
Or an allegory no doubt?"

Rose Renner

Why? I Don't Understand

Two little children playing on the swings
    Bright laughter fills the air!
    Eyes of blue and eyes of brown
One is dark, the other—so very fair

Two different families came to these shores
    One came with hopes and dreams
    The other bond in slavery
Separation, Fear, Pain, WAR—freedom—it seems

Time passes—Humanity matures and grows
    The park has one fountain
    The schools are segregated
Why is freedom so hard to obtain?

Two little children playing on the swings
    Bright laughter fills the air!
    One's future seems so bright
The other one still struggles. Is this fair?

Signed the Mother of the fair child
Rose Renner

1991

"Happy New Year"
There's an element in the air
That didn't used to be there

An element of anticipation

I feel it flowing everywhere
Sent to mine from God above

A hope For our futures at last

by Rose Renner

Hurricane Andrew

The power of the storm:
Unleashed was unconceivable.
Through miles and miles—home?
Nothing the same—everyone known gone.

The live wires everywhere
Metal beams twisted, concrete is torn.
Is our home still there?
Through miles and miles—trees upside down.

Is this the right street—strange?
Oh MY God, Look! The trailer park's gone!
Our community?
Destruction everywhere—My home?

Thank God! There's some walls—roof?
My son's room exploded—all gone.
The smell—the debris.
Where's This? Where's That? Where will we go?

by Rose Renner

Alone

No one to turn to—No where to go.
This world is a scary place, you know.

    Alone I face a new world
    Alone I care for my own
    The Hurricane Andrew came
    Destroyed our possessions, home.

Blond hair, blue eyes, a small hand in mine.
Pat her head. Tell her it will be fine.

    Though how much more can I live?
    Now we're up rooted again
    A single mother goes on
    Is there ever an end? When?
    I'm tired!

Rose Renner

Florida

Ocean waves, sand dunes, swaying palms
Take me home

Little lizards, southern pines, white tail deer
Take me home again

From the ocean thur the forest to the wetlands
I feel the pull

Couch shells, sand dollars, sandpipers
I feel the pull again

Waterways, clear lakes, orange groves
I want to go home

Great Herons, mangroves, quiet swamps
Home I Must go!

by Rose Renner

Maze of Life

Where am I in this maze of life?
What lies around this corner?
Is it the way out or the mynator?

I stand before the manger babe
Promise to heed the still small voice
He alone knows the way out near of far

The hopelessness I see today
Can't stay around much longer
Yet the complications weigh me down

The little one within can't die
The little one without cries
Where is the still small voice I need it's sound

Closer—endings—beginnings—when?
I can't go on much longer
The pain inside to strong to feel—heal me.

Rose Renner

A Man of Honor

A heart of Gold lies within
A man of strength I see

"Be the Best you can be"
His desire for you and me

A man of character
A man who needs to be

Intelligent, caring
But does he give too much?

If you give away your golden coins
They will but fade in their hands

Only what is earned
Can mankind see

"When the student is ready
The teacher will come"

Demand respect Sweetie
You've earned it!

Your Friend,
Rose

Miracle

There's a miracle unfolding
A dream coming true

A need for a new life
Spring is budding though

A reason for living A time for cheer

Tomorrow's a new day
Let go of fear.

There's a miracle unfolding A dream coming true

A time for beginning Let's start life anew!

By Rose Renner
6.5.92

The Pain

I awake in your arms
You are my constant friend
You never leave me!

Your caress is constant
Your touch, unforgetful
You will never flee

Tomorrow will I wake
To find peace or your love
To ever be?

Tonight I toss and turn
Comfort for one moment
Sleep, please find me

In my tummy and my head
I feel your presence
No one else sees

You are my silent lover

Rose Renner

Questions

Life and it's many mysterious turns

Throws questions in my head

What happened to yesterday's dreams
What will tomorrow be?

I must look to my Lord for guidance

By his hand, I'll be lead!

So many times I've wished to give up
Yet, He holds my hand tight

Yes, I've worried about tomorrow
And for what the future holds
Yet, what if tomorrow brings sorrow

Lord, let me desire to hold today
To enjoy it while I may
Least I lose an opportunity

Rose Renner

Reality

Reality is
Black and white
A few can see
The gray

* * * * *

But my world
Is Full of Colors
As Bright
As any Day!

* * * * *

The Light Beings
Surround Me
As Their Warmth
Fills My Air

* * * * *

The Harmony
Within
Is Balance
Created There

The Rose

Snowflakes

Snowflakes so softly floating down
Multitudes of individual designs
Tiny, delicate, not a sound
Picturesque hillsides—drawn with heavenly lines

Humanity ever seeking
Oh, multitudes of individual minds
Blowing with the wind—drifting
Stand your ground
   Quiet the mind
      Peace
         You will find

Humanity ever growing
Ever reaching, Ever seeking—The light is sent
Humanity ever children
Every single one
   So special
      So different

Snowflakes so softly floating down
Multitudes of individual designs
Tiny, delicate, not a sound
Picturesque hillsides—drawn in heavenly lines

The Rose

The Sailor's Heart

The mysterious Lady of the Sea
Awaits and beacons me.

From distant sandy island shores,
To iceberg legends of Viking lore.

From the tranquil Lady's loving demure
To her violent, vicious furor.

Should I stay here safe upon the shore?
Or venture out just once more?

The mysterious Lady of the Sea
Awaits and beacons me.

From distant sandy island shores…

by Rose Renner

Yesterday

Tomorrow is coming
I am not prepared
Must I release my dream
Of yesterday?
OR just the pain, it's hopes
Have brought to me?
Will that open a door
For it to be?
OR finally chase it from me?
I fight to hold on.
What happens when
I agree to let go?
Oh, Grandfather hold me!

By Rose Renner
1993

Thoughts of the Messenger

Thoughts of The Messenger

"Gabriel"—You are my oasis!

Harken Little ones
Children accept my Plea
For the night is not
Truly as dark as it seems!

"Now faith is the substance
of things hoped for,
The evidence of things not seen!"

What means the evidence of things not seen?
You can't see the wind. Yet what power can it contain?
Have you ever seen the results of a tornado?
Or a hurricane?

So what is faith?
"Something powerful that you can touch!"

Let Us Believe!

"Look unto the hills from whence cometh
your strength."

"Unto the hills" according to
The Strong's Concordance
was translated from a phrase meaning
a projection of power.

If "Christ" is within is not his power there also?

So if we look within to the projection
of the power of light,
We find our strength.

Know Thyself!

The Rose

Life is a school
Learn your lessons well
Or, you may repeat them!

"Worry not for lost knowledge
The Great Ones
Can send it when They Choose"

I'm weird
I'm different
I'm always alone

I'll bide my time
Seek unto me
MY OWN!

I do not fit in this realm!

My Family!

Isaiah 30:20-21
"In that day, you will hear and see your Teachers"

If they were walking around in churches or bodies
Isaiah would have been wasting his time
Telling us that we could hear and see them.

Prophets Do Not like to waste their time!

They are my family
I am never alone!

Rachel Weeps

A Mother without her child
Is like a dark night without stars!

Prophecy

Prophecy comes by area
So as we become one
In a global community
We must now seek all
To have a total view

Love

Love is but a way to learn,
Of peace and tranquility

The road is rough when confusion,
Stalks the heart of sincerity.

But love is strong and can heal the pain,
For it is the spark which creates the flame.

by Rose Renner
2.1987

Daddy's Favorite Poem

He who knows not and
Knows that he knows not
Is Simple—Teach him

He who knows not and
Knows not that he knows not
Is a Fool—Avoid him

He who knows and
Knows not that he knows
Is Asleep—Awaken him

But he who knows and
Knows that he knows is wise
Follow him!

                                    anonymous

Society

I am from a different place
How do I belong?
How do I learn to sing?
Society's song?

As winter comes upon the land
Remember the beauty of autumn leaves
Yet know that spring will come again
After the harsh winter breeze!

Power of the heavens
Energy of the ethers
Fullness of the moon

Colors of your aura
Wisdom of the teacher
Changes to come soon

Feel—Use—See—Know
Be Ready!

To Understand
The Simplicity
Of The Message

One Must First:

Begin to Comprehend
The Complexity
Of He Who Sent it!

Laugh With Life
Before It Laughs at You!

When life's pressures weigh you down
Remember who holds your hand

GOD won't let go of you Dear
Squeeze tight know that he is near

Life is Short
Yet
Life is Forever

God seems distant
Yet
God is Within

The pathway of the Rainbow
Contained in Pure white light
Holds the promise of Becoming

To commune soul to soul
To know as you know
To feel what you feel
To be one is real!

The Dream

"When you wish upon a star"
"A dream is a wish the heart makes"
or should we…
"Release the butterfly and
If it returns it is yours;
If not it never was."
And just concern ourselves to:
"Follow the yellow brick road"

Time

What was to be
Can not you see
Time changes things:
Different paths have been taken
Different worlds shaken
Time changes things
But I have not bent to time

March 21, 1993

To survive or to live
One must learn to know
The secrets of his soul

To become is a gift of old
To let go is to be free

I Don't Believe in Excuses

If you're right, you don't need them
If you are wrong, they don't help!

I am a Complete Woman

A complete woman is like
A highly polished diamond.

She has many polished faucets
Which all face in totally different directions.

No one in this realm has ever seen
All of my faucets!

A voice I hear,
"If you give away your golden coins
they will but fade in their hands
A truth is only a truth
If it comes from within"!

The Aura is vibrations from thought
As pebbles dropped in a pond
Send ringlets out to it's shore

God is Big—Man is Little!
Deal with it!

When you are backed into a corner
With no way out but up
Thank—God
For the opportunity
To draw closer
To your Creator!

Be Ye Prefect

A command Yeshua gave
We were not asked to try

As Yoda told Skywalker
"Do not try just do" Sigh

Okay, that's hard, that hits home

My kids are worth every gray hair
They've given me
I just don't see any reason
To show it!

Never waste a Dream!
If you're going to dream
Dream Big!

I am an imperfect vessel
But aren't we all?

Messages and Future

The Goat

Remember the Goat
Who leads the sheep to Slaughter?
When he comes, will you know him?

He's a great leader
He wears the color of white
It's his job to protect them

Isn't he the Sheppard?
The sheep follow willingly
Even though the narrow gate

The Slaughter house awaits
The pathway winds so softly
Will they know before to late?

Nope

By The Messenger

Change

Serapis is waiting
Moses is setting up blocks
Peter is climbing the hill

Shaman are flying as eagles
Spirits are leaving this world

Mankind must learn balance
In their body, mind and soul

Natures demands are higher
It's truth we must enfold

Power of the heavens
Energy of the ethers
Fullness of the moon

Colors of the aura
Wisdom of Morya
Changes to come soon
Feel—Use—See—Know
Be Ready

Tomorrow will come what may

by The Messenger

Earth Changes

As a dog shakes off water, this planet will remove its dark cloud.

This life-wave has created a shadow cloud surrounding itself.

As Earth awakes she will feel the heavy cloak you've laid upon her.

She can not breathe. Its weight becomes more each day. It follows her everywhere.

Tomorrow she will awaken to clear the air and force off the cloak.

Hold fast my little ones. Send out light to lighten her load.

When the cloud dissipates, we can rise together.

Rainbows, sunshine, fresh air, clean water
A new day awaits you,

Hold tight for just a little while.

The Messenger

Friends

Long Ago-Far Away,
    In a distant time unknown,
I lived in another place!

The land was red and deserted.
    The sky had no air.
We dwelt in caverns.

The survivors of an ancient catastrophe,
    That had blown
Atmosphere and surface out.

But, peace reigned,
    And intelligence and love abounded there.
In comparison, Earth fails.

Pain of a distant past,
    Forged a future filled with hope,
As we lie dying in space.

Our neighbor so little, so blue,
    Leads a dangerous life.
They grow in hatred and war.

Observant we watch the signs,
    Desiring to help them cope.
We get involved one by one.

Hot sun, green grass, tall trees, new bodies,
    A world of strife.
How to teach Love and Peace?

So many lifetimes,
    Have come and gone in this land.
We helped to shape your history.

Existent in your life wave,
    Til eternity ends.
Our souls can not go home.

We became one with you,
    To love and be hand in hand.
Put away your war. Learn peace.

The time has come to grow.
    Learn the lessons God sends.
He is the same EVERYWHERE!

By The Rose

I See a Cave

I see a very large cave
So much equipment
Computers, Dialysis machine

Two entrances—very long tunnels
One is a back door to Pakistan
The other intersected by a tunnel.

Many people are here
Then I see outside in Pakistan
A small village, here he is a lord

Then I see a hiding place
After the cave, a long empty road
At the edge of a huge valley

I only see one small tree
About five small homes
A few up against the mountains

In one of them he can hide

The Messenger

Mankind

Oh, how little is your God?
What has been
Can be again.

The Light Ones DO speak!
It is not channeling
They can be in more places than one.

Balance is needed now
Heed their plea
Balance will come if we don't create it.

The Rose

Peace

An apple on a barren tree
The fruit of a new age

Open your eyes and see
We're the beginning of a page

> The secrets of the distant past
> May be ours at last

> First comes the peace
> Always the love
> Forever the friendship

How do we make it happen?
Where do we go for aid?

Oh, but our prayers to send
The One by whom we've become

> And they who are above
> Wish to lead the way in love.

By Rose Renner
9.23.86

Secrets

For thousands of eons,
        The secrets have been kept.
Million of men proven,
        While more billions have slept.

Yet, there aren't eons left.
        Decisions must be made.
Should the doors be opened?
        Or secrets kept forbade?

Let's open them slightly,
        Guarding deepest depths.
One soul's enlightenment,
        And our answer's been met!

By The Rose

The Sandbox

Here I sit viewing the sandbox,
    Through a one way mirror.
God's children still fighting,
    Some filled with fear.
Our sandbox is weakening.
    How long will it last?
Our Teacher is calling.
    Please, listen to him fast!
Many small ones are pushing.
    The bully's there too.
The one in the middle,
    wears red, white and blue.
He must Stop the pushing.
    Show the bully his strength.
So determined to be peacemaker,
    But to what length?
They need to mature.
    There's so much more to life,
Then fighting and famine,
    Brought on by so much strife.
If he followed the Teacher,
    Would they not go too?
The bully's such a foe.
    He's afraid to go!

The darkness is falling.
The light is calling.

Will they follow the Teacher,
        to the light?
Or will they fight,
        the pestilence of the night?
Their sandbox is shaking.
        Will it be too late?

Or will the Teacher call for others,
To Physically STOP all this hate?!

by Rose Renner

The Unborn One

As told by the prophet of old
        Your arrival will be known

The dragon awaited your birth
        After you'd raised from the earth

In the wilderness she did pray
        The lady counted the days

Rachel's crying for her children
        It states they will be returned

He'll be the king with the iron fist
        He's the Light One sent from high

Barabas he was called before
        And also Cedric the Third

When the Merovingians lost France
        He came back to aid their cause

In a monastery he died
        His mission to his people lost

Today he awaits to return
        His spirit caught up to God

The dark one wants to steal his heart
            To twist his mind, rape his soul

They created lies to take her
            Special one's gone from us

She will return and he will come
            God's big and man is little!

"Revenge is mine the Lord saith"
            Hurricanes ravage that state

His name Nathaniel David
            He'll wear the mark I've been told

The protector will arrive soon
            He's taking so very long

The lady carries his body
            The Creator protects his soul

They will unite when time is right
            Lady "prays without ceasing!"

The Messenger

Send the Warrior

Dear tiny, little one within,
      Slight movements on my spine.
Who will help me open the door,
      To let you free in this time?

How to hold you in my arms,
      To touch your face, feel your charm?

Great Spirit heed the circle of light.
      Come to us in our night.
Send the warrior of your choice,
      Grant him compassion and sight!

Until then we cry alone,
      Fighting to survive on our own.

So many secrets I must bare,
      Without anyone to care.
Time passes as it may,
      Ever cautious of dawning day.

Hope can never grow to dim,
      For LIGHT brings balance within!

by The Rose

Love

From many past lifetimes
Your face I see.

From child to God
You've been to me.

Though life and death
You'll ever be!

My past—our past
Pathways entwined

How do I answer
The questions of your soul?

How do I give
The things you need to know

SEEK an Ye shall FIND

Rose

Biloxi

September 29, 2004

A dream I remember
Concerning possible sites
For a terrorist attack

I was doing research
An Internet newsletter
I was to write, I searched for facts

Then

I saw devastation
It was as far as I could see
No trees, buildings, just debris

"Biloxi"

A voice I did hear speak
I suddenly awakened
I still see the land, debris

"Camille"

Confused, I find myself
In bed, looking at my clock
A warning I'd been given

Terrorists, Act of God
Which shall it be? How do I warn?
What intricate message woven?

What shall be will be

The Messenger

The Golden Gate Bridge

After Katrina came ashore
My thoughts went to Atlanta
Now, before Iraqi Freedom
I'd seen it hit three times

After passing on my vision
To both sides of the aisle
Two hundred shoulder guns at
Marta Train Station did find

Then in two thousand and four
God lead me to Atlanta
Realized what the three were
Of course I passed it on

I thought we'd stopped it, but no
I heard it will happen if
This country doesn't obey
Laws of God I'd passed on

Yes, I thought of Atlanta
Then heard, "No, San Francisco"
I refused to believe what heard
It's hard to pass on bad

Sometimes you don't want to hear
I saw the Golden gate Bridge
Terrorist or natural?
It just leaves my heart sad

Visions

To see and not to see all
Leaves one in despair

Day after day, time slips by
Pain within I care

Yet I've passed the message on
Will that change anything?

Is the future just foretold?
Or what can hope bring

Suddenly time happens
Now I understand

The puzzle is complete
As I view the land

Must innocents always die?

The Messenger

Reincarnation

The Christ said John the Baptist was Elias
John the Baptist said he wasn't

Should I need to choose
I'd choose the Christ over the forerunner

So as a layperson
All I can conclude is

Just because you know you ain't
It don' mean you aren't

Maybe The Creator has more mercy
Than you've given Him credit for?

And remember,
Who someone was is never as important
As what they do today with who they are

The Rose